Waiting for the Wood Thrush

poems by

Ashley Memory

Finishing Line Press
Georgetown, Kentucky

Waiting for the Wood Thrush

For Johnpaul

Love's not Time's fool, though rosy lips and cheeks
Within his bending sickle's compass come;
Love alters not with his brief hours and weeks,
But bears it out even to the edge of doom.
—William Shakespeare, from *Sonnet 116*

"This being human is a guest house. Every morning a new arrival. A joy, a depression, a meanness, some momentary awareness as an unexpected visitor.... Be grateful for whoever comes, because each has been sent as a guide from beyond."
—Rumi

Copyright © 2019 by Ashley Memory
ISBN 978-1-64662-010-4 First Edition
All rights reserved under International and Pan-American Copyright Conventions. No part of this book may be reproduced in any manner whatsoever without written permission from the publisher, except in the case of brief quotations embodied in critical articles and reviews.

ACKNOWLEDGMENTS

Many thanks to the editors of the following journals in which these poems first appeared.

Broad River Review: "Why I Love Used Books" (Spring 2016)

Coffin Bell: "Orchard #9" (January 2019)

Indy Week: "How to See a Ghost" (April 2014)

Naugatuck River Review: "The Murder House on Sweetwater Ridge" (Finalist in the 2015 Narrative Poetry Contest)

Pinesong: "Phalaenopsis", "Napoleon and Antosia" (2015) and "A Widow on Chester Street" (2016)

Poetry in Plain Sight Project, Winston-Salem Writers: "Consider the Spider" (July 2018)

Turnpike Magazine: "Ode to the Goddess of Missing Tools" and "Self-Portrait of the Stunt Double for Vivien Leigh" (March 2019)

Publisher: Leah Maines
Editor: Christen Kincaid
Cover Art: Johnpaul Harris
Author Photo: Johnpaul Harris
Cover Design: Elizabeth Maines McCleavy

Printed in the USA on acid-free paper.
Order online: www.finishinglinepress.com
        also available on amazon.com

Author inquiries and mail orders:
Finishing Line Press
P. O. Box 1626
Georgetown, Kentucky 40324
U. S. A.

Table of Contents

Phalaenopsis 1

The Prince of Someday 2

Why J.P. Dreamt of a Naked Ghost Named Rebecca 3

Waiting for the Wood Thrush 4

One Thousand Octobers 5

The Murder House at Sweetwater Ridge 6

Consider the Spider 8

Elisabeth 9

Orchard #9 11

Self-Portrait as Stunt Woman for Vivien Leigh Falling
    Down the Stairs in *Gone with the Wind* 14

A Widow on Chester Street 15

Eulogy of the Northern Red Oak 17

Ode to the Goddess of Lost Tools 19

Napoleon and Antosia 20

Old Pine Door 21

Lost and Found of the Dead 22

Samarcand 25

You're Not Invited 26

Why I Love Used Books 27

Little Girl Buried in Rum Keg 28

How to See a Ghost 30

Too Bad You Were Never Mine 32

Best Price Sin Town 33

Phalaenopsis

My window is framed
by a jabot of white blossoms
each petal stained with drops
of red-violet ink.

People walking by gasp with delight
or is it surprise that someone so silly
and disorganized would own
such a perfect thing?

What they don't see is what I know:
in the wild forest of my life
there now dwells a rogue
symmetry.

A gift, said a co-worker
for what I considered to be
the smallest of favors.

I think people are like
orchids, delicate and brave
giving back in beauty
what we give them in
kindness.

The Prince of Someday

Our friend Harmon dwells in the streets
of by and by, safe from the cruelty
of deadlines and the possibility
his dreams might come to naught.

He thinks he'll hike Mauna Loa
plant an orchard of paw-paw trees
or better yet, host a weekly *tête-à-tête*
for people who also like to talk.

He wants to build a spiral staircase,
weave a vest from porcupine quills.
Line a screen porch in fresh cedar
Knot a hammock by hand.

Priorities, priorities, we're prone to nag,
legs crossed in his cluttered studio
weary of holding it until we get home.
What if you started with indoor plumbing?

Ironically, he's a master of superrealism
Each painting a study in the finest of detail
this blade of grass, that butterfly wing
a mouse that appears to quiver.

What others call procrastination,
this modern day sin, is for Harmon
an act of faith, a belief in the power
of another morning.

Secretly we envy our golden friend,
for while we all scramble for a toehold
on the mountain, Harmon climbs cheerfully,
tethered to an invisible net of hope.

Why J.P. Dreamt of a Naked Ghost Named Rebecca

Her nakedness, we think, came from a favorite book
The Nude, A Study in Ideal Form by Kenneth Clark,
who tells us even though we've flung aside the mantle
of ancient Greece, the nude lives on.

About Rebecca, maybe because we just watched
Brideshead Revisited with an elderly Laurence Olivier
and thought of his youthful brilliance as Max de Winter
in the movie of the same name?

Or is it because the dogs of a distant neighbor
named Becky—who manages the DMV tag office—
have started roaming our yard and peeing
on our scalawag holly bush?

Instead I wonder if he's haunted by a lover
from his past, a chic goddess who waters
his loofah seedlings bare-breasted,
like *Aphrodite de Melos*.

I remember the words of a French Quarter fortune
teller who once held my hand and murmured
*Tell me what you dream and I'll tell you
who you are.*

Now J.P. asks, maybe to console,
maybe to detract, will you ever forget the climax
of that movie, when Laurence Olivier tells
Joan Fontaine he really *hated* Rebecca?

Waiting for the Wood Thrush

Breath of spring has sprung
vanilla petals lost to wind
Squirrels dash and bicker
frogs peep and peep again.

Cardinals preen *pretty, pretty*
Woodpeckers hammer until noon.
Honeybees hobnob round the plum
and crickets trill to the moon.

What we don't yet hear this spring
is the voice of the shy passerine
beguiling us from the bramble
a speckled breast never seen.

He may sire a brood or not
but he never stays too long.
From May to August he haunts
with his peculiar eerie song.

The descant to spring's melody
those footprints in the dew
God, a whisper: *Come to me.
Here I am. Right near you.*

One Thousand Octobers

One thousand Octobers would never be enough.
Still I ask, why didn't we meet before?
You bring pears in the first blush of our love,
and drop your mask when I open up the door.

I think sometimes that we did meet before,
still, all the wasted years, nights spent alone . . .
I drop my mask when you open up the door
and wave goldenrod upon a fairy stone.

All the wasted years, nights spent alone
yearning for each other, thirsty at the well …
We lay goldenrod upon a fairy stone,
trade ghost stories, the nectar in our spell.

On our second date we kissed at the well,
and at dusk we read the poetry of Keats.
Our ghosts swirl in cider, notes of caramel,
we dance in an orchard of moon-dappled streets.

Soon we married, a fate cruelly denied to Keats…
We nibble on pears when we celebrate our love
and dance in an orchard of moon-dappled streets.
One thousand Octobers would never be enough.

The Murder House at Sweetwater Ridge

What would you say if you knew
the house you so proudly built
for your bride now drifts in
a thicket of blackjack, red
cedar and chickweed?

But the towhee still sings
drink your tea and the
sparrow calls back
please pretty please
Purple thistle bobs with
painted ladies and the air is sweet
with wild raspberries

And at night the fireflies bounce
off the white clover like stars
falling to earth.

What would you say if you knew
the porch where you waited
for your bride to come home
that last day has crumbled and
fallen away?

What would you say if you knew
they still talk about how you cradled your bride
after you shot her and had her blood
on your hands when you went inside
to end it all?

What would you say if you knew
your house is now called the murder house
and that some kids snuck inside one
night with spray paint and left handprints
in red for all to see?

What would you say if you knew
her family wouldn't bury
her next to you so she sleeps
with her own kin under a stone that says
too good for this world?

What would you say if you knew
the house you so proudly built
for your bride now drifts in
a thicket of blackjack, red
cedar and chickweed?

But the towhee still sings
drink your tea and the
sparrow calls back
please pretty please
Purple thistle bobs with
painted ladies and the air is sweet
with wild raspberries

And at night the fireflies bounce
off the white clover like stars
falling to earth.

Consider the Spider

How she trapezes between the hibiscus
and parsley then spirals her lair
against the nacreous light
of a crescent moon.

We swing weary legs
in the breeze, wonder what
happened to the day—new ditch
not yet cut, river rock still
unshoveled, laundry on
the line—and marvel
at the industry of the tiny
amber acrobat.

Oh, the chances we would take if
our lives depended on it.

Elisabeth

We never met the woman who lived
at 87 Rue des Martyrs in Montmartre—
a road they say St. Denis climbed in 250 A.D.,
severed head in hand.

We connected on the internet,
once there greeted by her son Alain,
who, after a lecture on water conservation,
tosses us a brass skeleton key.

Curiosities surround us—
rumors of Brazilian transvestites
erratic hours of *La Poste*, those divine
éclairs at the corner pâtisserie—yet

we're fascinated by the chic homeowner:
her grass broom, naturopathy magazines
a photo of a man in a turtleneck
walking in snow—*Antoine, mon chéri.*

In a leather journal embossed with an E,
that same taut hand pens rules:
La cigarette? Non, dans la maison.
Oui, sur le balcon.

In the kitchen: wine, white and trendy rosé
a jar of olives, honey from Corsica,
ketchup in the fridge, *humm*, is it hers or
is it for *les Americains?*

Her taste in books ranges from the
literary—Flaubert and Melville—
to the erotic, with meditations on
the art of the caress.

She's not there, I know, but whenever
we walk through the front door
a trench coat on a hanger rakes the wood,
stirs a tiny breeze of Chanel No. 5.

It's as if she waits on the balcony
where she flicks ashes in a tray,
and deluded by wine, wonders
if the clatter is her Antoine, home at last.

Orchard #9

Welcome to Jessup Family Orchard
spells crude crimson letters on wormy plywood.
Cherries, says Joe to Lily. *Wouldn't that be nice?*
But we came for a fresco, she reminds him

fanning herself with a map limp from worry.
She would have prayed to the Virgin
if the door to St. Ann's hadn't been barred.
We need a miracle.

Grim, Joe accelerates, the Wagoneer
groans as they climb the mountain.
Rhododendron heads sway then sneer
but in a glade flashes the face of a little girl.

When Lily looks again sycamore
and paulownia leaves fold to darkness.
Why, why, why ponders a crow,
arcing across a lavender sky.

Frank Jessup dribbles tobacco into a cup,
waves an arm toward Orchard #8.
The girl! cries Lily. *Did I see a girl?*
No, he snaps. *Just me and Ma.*

A woman in a wheelchair, hands macraméd
with blue veins, turns a mug in her lap.
Sweet churries all froze out, she croaks.
Plenty of sour, make you a nice pie.

Gnarled trees scabbed with lichen huddle
on the hill like knock kneed wizards.
Lily shudders while Joe shimmies up
a ladder, tousles branches until

hard red-orange orbs plop
like stones into a bucket.
Lily's teeth pierce flesh so sour
her cheeks dimple, tongue curls.

Jam, says Joe, spewing.
They'll make good jam.

Notes of *Little Deuce Coupe*
his favorite whistle, drift below.

Let it go, he'd snarled at breakfast, slashing
toast with cold butter. *We're too old for a baby.*
You don't know what it feels like, she'd spat,
grazing her elbow on the hot griddle.

Garroted by spider silk, Lily trudges on,
ripping cherries from low branches.
An empty bucket pops against her hip
as she strews her pickings to squirrels.

Legs lashed by briars, weary with thirst
eyes blinded by sun, she crumples.
The crow arcs again, teases *Make a pie…*
pie, pie, pie, before dipping over the hill.

Numb, Lily follows, as if in a trance.
The hill rolls into a valley, studded with trees
sinewy and lush, rising like nosegays.
They bulge with red-violet cabochons

so plump they crackle, ooze juice.
Beside Lily stands the girl. *Hello.*
Half-sprite, half-waif, she curtsies.
My name is Alunda.

A plait of brown hair swishes across a shoulder
puffed with lace, a ragged hem bobs along the grass.
A tangle of clover and thistle crowns her head,
sticky fingers offer cherries.

Ravenous, Lily sucks them into her mouth.
Honey, notes of mint, melancholia.
Did she whisper it or did Lily just know?
Sweet cherries always grow in #9.

Silver eyes water but do not blink.
Take all you like, Alunda says.
Lily, once sated, drops to her knees.
Alunda sighs, weaving clover with thistle.

Are you lonely too? Lily asks.
Alunda, somber, presents a garland
she threads through Lily's hair.
Take me home, she murmurs.

Leaves crimp, feathers crunch
as the crow floats from the tree.
He fixes an ice-blue eye on Lily,
tilts to Alunda, then coos *My, my, my.*

Lily lays her head on moss, closes her eyes.
Could that gurgle be a brook in the glen?
A cool hand strokes her forehead.
Take me home, Alunda says again.

The sound of her name falls like a hammer
cracking the peace of her reverie.
When she opens her eyes, Joe hovers,
his hand in hers. *Where have you been?*

Number 9, Lily says, touching her hair.
But the clover is gone, her bucket, empty.
Dehydrated, says Joe. *That's all.*
He tugs at her lips, offers water.

Only 8 orchards here, grunts Frank.
He snubs the money offered by Joe,
instead pulls Lily to her feet.
You'll be on your way now.

In the Wagoneer three heads bounce
down the mountain. *Alunda!* cries Ma.
Hush, says Frank. *For the best....*
But the old woman sobs on.

The crow circles round, pulsing higher and higher
through whip-stitched clouds, a final sally.
Frank's voice cracks, an echo of the old bird.
Good-bye, he mumbles. *Bye, bye, bye.*

Self-Portrait as Stunt Woman for Vivien Leigh Falling Down the Stairs in *Gone with the Wind*

> *"I was black and blue for a while. But I knew how to fall."*
> – Stuntwoman Addie Hash Warp (in 2005 at age 91).

You can spin the horn
even ride Roman style
What the hell's wrong
with you taunts Mr. Fleming
ridiculous I know but
still I teeter on
that third
step.

Gable coolly smokes a cigarette
Viv whispers *you're my favorite*
because you're little like me
and then there's Hattie who
teases, hums *Sooner or Later*.
Thoughts whirl, collide and I'm back
in Grass County, Montana where
little brother Joe says I lie like
a suck-egg dog when I say
I'm not scared.

Then I'm sitting on the bitterroot
under the constellation of Leo
with the one-armed cowboy who
says if I go to Hollywood he might
not be here when I come back.

Now there's Mama
who says *Buck up, girl*
so I close my eyes,
let go, softly, softly,
and we roll Mason
jars full of cream down
Crazy Mountain
nothing breaks and
at the end there's
butter, pure butter.

A Widow on Chester Street

Lucie Mae Moffitt cried, God help her she cursed, the family
of Japanese beetles squatting on her red hibiscus tree.

Giddy, some even swung upside down like the clip-on earring she lost
on the Ferris wheel at the state fair in 1977.

From his glider Herman would've chuckled now as he chuckled then.
No use crying over spilt milk. Ministers think like that.
Lucie Mae does not.

Neighbors peeked through jalousies as she whooshed three beetle traps
down her clothesline. *Might as well hand-deliver invitations,*
tsk-tsked Mary Alice.

A day later someone dubbed Edna's Rose of Sharon the Ghost of Sharon.
But nobody snickered when the beetles doilied Duncan's flowering crab.

Next they crocheted Abigail's grape vine and just for kicks they chewed up
and spit out Bobby Joe's pittosporum. Peter's purple leaf plum? Pulverized.

Over a pot of tizzy tea, Lucie Mae fretted until her pin curls unraveled.
A beetle bungeed into her chinoiserie cup. She stood.
Time to peel off the lace gloves.

Leave well enough alone, the glider would've uttered.
But by then Lucie was whirring toward Lane's Nursery
in her navy blue Lincoln Continental.

Deliver to Chester Street! she commanded, snagging the last five hibiscus
trees. Card? Indeed. Courtesy of Lucie Mae Moffitt.

Too far? Lucie Mae wondered over a cup of mea culpa tea.
For once the glider didn't speak. *No use,* she half-chuckled
half-trembled, *crying over spilt milk.*

Two days later she woke to the *put-it-here, put-it-there* of Eastern blue birds
as plump as pin cushions. Cardinals and chickadees sashayed in next.

Avian occupancy soared and people migrated to Chester Street to swoon
over the double-decker nest boxes. No binoculars needed. Umbrellas
advised.

If the sky falls, Lucie Mae said to *The Herald* reporter, a boy far too young to know what it meant to let go, *better just hold up your hands.*

Eulogy of the Northern Red Oak
Cedar Grove Fire District, N.C.
1952-2017

You hooked a hairy toe
in terracotta clay the same year
Lilibet's head wobbled
under the weight of a crown.

In 1967, when the world
first heard Sgt. Pepper's,
young bucks circled your trunk,
rubbed velvet from their antlers
yet you still raced to the sky.

Lightning whipped, then singed you in 1981,
after a madman shot the Pope
but he lived, and so did you.

As sunlight parted the Berlin Wall in 1989,
a clearwing borer drilled a lodge
only an itch under your alligator mantle.

In 1993 when loggers roared in and sawed down your family,
you sighed, then spread your limbs and danced
as Al Pacino won an Oscar for *Scent of a Woman*.

In your new wedge of sun, fresh leaves
unfurled daily, absinthe to the squirrels
a bower for the secret summer tanager.

You celebrated the millennium with your own seed
which bounced on the roof like firecrackers
but we still bought the house,
planted begonias around you.

The winter of 2002 with its snow and ice
crippled dogwoods and a hickory, yet you thrived,
even basked in the glow of the Geminids.

Soon you towered over sycamore and white oak cousins
Your shadow purpled the old trading path and ancient yucca . . .
Lord of the Uwharries, did you know your days were numbered?

In June 2017 we told ourselves you breathed too close
to the house but in truth we craved
more sun for our beefsteak tomatoes.

When you fell, the earth didn't shake as long as it should have.
We'll be all right, we kidded ourselves, as we rolled you to the burn pile
and kindled your branches to fire.

The earth shook again weeks later
when we raked the grass around your stump
our fingers folded a cradle of twigs
inside, the skeleton of a baby tanager
with a broken neck.

Ode to the Goddess of Lost Tools

A minor deity, so inconsequential she
never had a name or a temple, yet
her powers rival those of Zeus and Hera.
She strikes where it hurts the most.

Naughtier than Pan, she snatches
not just any of your 7 drills but
the DeWalt 20-Volt Cordless,
leaving you bereft and idle.

She loves to purloin pipe cutters,
particularly the ½-inch size,
the one you need now, only to
hide it later in your Jetta.

When she dances in the moonlight
we know she wields Grandfather's hammer
paint-spattered, hickory handle—
your proudest possession.

Is that rain or wind, we ask
on a summer night though
we know what we hear
is the echo of her laughter.

She can't turn anything to gold
or make anyone immortal but
when she steals, she also befuddles,
thwarting recovery.

Look, you say, emerging from the basement,
the chisel long-forgotten. Your eyes dance
and your hand spans a DVD. *Rita Hayworth
in The Lady from Shanghai!*

Napoleon and Antosia

> *Two passionate donkeys separated because of an outcry over their lovemaking have been reunited at a zoo in Poland.*
> ~ Associated Press in Warsaw

For a moment he didn't recognize her because
when they brought her back she did not swing
her tail the way she used to and her eyes did not

shine. He put his head over her neck and inhaled the
tang of clover mixed with barley straw—the scent of
his Silly-Face—the jenny who'd once poked her head

through a dewy spider web and looked up at him
with a coronet of jewels. But still he wondered.
Had she found another Splashy-Mouth?

When the keeper-he-used-to-like gave her an apple
again would she walk away for good this time?
The first night was not the worst; she had been

gone that long before, but then there was a second
and a third and a fourth and then he lost count
because he passed over the threshold of forever

Now that she is back, he notices the gawkers
around the pen, people he had never thought
about before because they had been like the trees

nothing more. Now they are loud in a bad way, smelling
of bad things and their stares and their laughter hurt.
He used to live for the nights when he and Silly-Face

were alone in the world but since coming back from
forever even though they gaze at the same sky
he knows they see
different
moons.

Old Pine Door

Strewn across a bare field bordered by
red barns and pastures, Liberty Antiques Fair
offers hand-me-downs from the ages,
personal and industrial.

A basket of assorted doll arms and legs
two-man chain saw, kiddie carnival cars
hand-powered gas pump, cider mills
postcards from Lookout Mountain
and Skyline Drive where people write
of fine times, wish you were here.

Good-natured haggling rules,
sprinkled with memories of Bubble-Up
soft drink and a '36 Packard.

Only a farmer from Denton holds
fast to $125 for a prized door from
his grandfather's 1914 farm.

Six panels of solid pine, never painted
original lock set, porcelain knob
door to the Sunday House, where
guests spent the night when the
big house overflowed.

At 4 p.m., when dazed shoppers
walk out with their weather vanes,
stained glass, Mobil Oil signs,
quilt racks and wrench sets,
Mr. Bobby Lee Ferguson holds
tight to his door, at least until tomorrow
Won't go any lower, he says,
biting his lip.

Lost and Found of the Dead

A wave of sour mop and gloom washes
over you inside 92 West Main, same
grim building where people pay fines,
file complaints about the city.

You spring down the steps to the basement
heart eased by the light-hearted dare
that led you here. *I don't think you've
got the nerve,* teased a friend.

The metal door to Room 07B swings
open easily, yet the creak whinnies
like a lonely horse, and for no reason
an old hymn seeps through your mind.

*Though none go with me
I still will follow
No turning back,
no turning back.*

Inside the windowless room
the air whispers of old pennies, tinged
with antiseptic. A dirty fluorescent light
flickers over a man at a desk.

He raises watery eyes to yours
turns a head of yellow-gray hair
offers the curtest of nods.
L.C. Hearn. Can I help you?

Where's the emeralds? you ask,
trying to be funny. *What about
the lost Rembrandt? Cats waiting
to be mummified?*

You feel stupid because you realize
he must hear these things all the time.
Of course he doesn't laugh,
your pony-tailed Charon rows on.

Those things are upstairs, he says,
in the Unclaimed Property Department.
He jams glasses up his nose,
rolls away from the desk.

With surprising energy, he opens drawer
after drawer, each one labeled by hand:
*Second Thoughts, Broken Promises,
Pointless Arguments,* even *Idle Gossip,*

surely a minor vice, a victimless crime....
You want to ask, but don't, scared of the answer:
*Do the dead ever show up and claim these things?
How do you know what belongs to whom?*

Instead you peer into *Unrequited Love,*
and it's dark inside but overflows with the sound
of true melancholy: a slur of notes that ends
on a low whistle, spirals on and on and on....

Ballad of a bird who never finds a mate
Sighs of lovers parted by distance and time
flutter of letters never mailed
scent of wilted lilacs over lichen.

L.C. grunts, his eyes now gleam pewter,
and he rolls to a cabinet that spans the wall.
What no one can believe. He waves you over,
opens the drawer to *Apologies.*

You drown in a million little murmurs,
susurrus of ghosts, messages in bottles
that still float in the sea, endless echo
of unspoken words thwarted by pride.

Woozy, you wade through your own regrets,
countless times you should have said *I'm sorry.*
To the ninth grade teacher you mocked
to the classmate who walked too slow.

To your mother, whose calls roll to voicemail
more often than not—is it really important?
For the dinners you should have cooked for her.
To the driver of the blue Hyundai you cut off

this morning, too busy to yield.
To your fiancé and the many arguments
that just fritter away before you
take your share of the blame.

What people don't realize, L.C. says,
as if talking to himself, *is that
apologies don't cost a damn cent.*
Your face burns scarlet with shame

because you think the same thing.
He averts his eyes, clears his throat.
*It's time for my lunch and I have to lock up.
You can come back at 2 if...*

No, no, you mumble, having seen enough.
You take the survey card he presses in your hand,
marvel at the absurdity. *How are we doing?
Tell us how we can improve service to you!*

Outside the sun blazes, much brighter
than before, the prediction for rain
a mistake, everyone around you
bounces with glee.

A whistling man walks a schnauzer,
a young mother smiles at him then you,
the twins in her stroller laugh at the dog
even the crossing guard nods his head.

Have you been to 92 West Main
you want to shout, even to the
lollipop-waving toddlers. *Room 07B!
Go now, before it's too late.*

But they hurry on,
and so do you, even as
you shudder in the shadow
of 92 West Main.

You want to be happy, too,
you want to hum a light tune
but all ditties dissolve
into that same old hymn.

*Though none go with me
I still will follow
No turning back,
no turning back.*

Samarcand

> "A homelike place where those who have fallen may find temporary shelter, and under a firm yet kind discipline, begin to live morally."
> – North Carolina State Archives, Samarcand Manor, 1918-2011

Peach orchards ripple
through the Sandhills
in the shadow of a manor
where they reformed poor girls
made to garden and weave.

In July, at Whitacre's Variety Stand,
suede pink moons nestle in boxes
wooed by yellow jackets
who threaten, then drown
in the nectar of the blems.

A girl, same age as the ones
who rebelled in 1931, offers
a Fire Prince, rumored better,
she says, with a flip of her braid,
than a Windblow.

She twirls it open with her hands,
tiny red teeth surrender aurelian flesh
and the juice spritzes my arm—
sticky perfume of dew-fed grass
clover honey, even cinnamon,
the elixir of dreams—
what Samarcand robbed
from the girls.

It must be hard to work here
I prattle, as my thoughts drift to jam,
cobblers, and tarts. *So much temptation!*
The girl leans over as she wipes
her hands. *I don't care for peaches,
never have.*

You're Not Invited

Seconds before the words sailed out of her mouth
it was like any other Saturday in June—I sat cross-legged
under the magnolia while my best friend French-braided my hair—
and she'd brought up the pizza outing so casually
I assumed I would go, too, but now I swayed, dizzied
by the weight of teenaged awkwardness, chicken legs,
lips puckered by braces, rosacea-dappled cheeks
and she felt it, too, the taut braid unfurls, she starts again,
stammers *Sorry, sorry, sorry, of course you can go* . . . .
but even now, at my first child's christening,
her father's funeral, our twenty-year reunion, the words
draw between us like a cheap curtain, too flimsy
to block the sun but a wall nonetheless,
words she can't take back
words that make me forever wonder
if the others at the mimosa bar, staff meeting,
even the check-out line at Harris Teeter,
wish I wasn't there.

Why I Love Used Books

Leafing through Perrine's *Sound and Sense*
the handwriting of Jeannette Venable scrawls
like Whitman's noiseless and patient spider.
Was she a poet, I wonder, perhaps a student?

Religious, no doubt, judging from circled passages
of John Donne and Gerard Manley Hopkins.
She pens a sad face by Arnold's *Dover Beach*
Only a return to truth will save us, she muses.

She scoffs at the mudliciousness of e.e. cummings
Not for me, she scribbles, and the verse of Sylvia Plath
perplexes because here she is strangely silent.
The Spinster, I imagine, squeezes a nerve.

Even though on page 41 the highlighter draws
a pink line through *The purest form of practical language
is the scientific,* I know that a romantic lives
at Cashew Court, #45A, in Clio, California.

Ahh, she writes beside the villanelle of Collins
Why can't goodbye come back to hello?
A single tear warps Browning's *Sonnet 14*
If thou must love me, let it be for nought.

In the glossary, she checks off haiku,
stars *masculine rhyme,* and questions *triple meter.*
When the highlighter runs through *understatement*
I know that Jeannette is a poet after all.

Jeannie, reads a yellowed index card
tucked in the middle. *Sorry I missed you.
Couldn't pass up the job in Portland.
Fondly, Phil.*

Little Girl Buried in Rum Keg

For most of Ms. Burkhart's
fourth grade class Plot #24
in Beaufort's Old Burying Ground
delights and relieves.

They've already bounced on the British
soldier buried upright in his boots
imagined the monkey barrel
of bones in the mass grave

of sailors who drowned when
the *Crissie Wright* ran ashore.
They rubbed the enemy cannon
mounted on the brick tomb

of 1812 hero Otway Burns.
Only Alex Ryan dared scramble
on top and giddy-up, even to the
tut-tuts of Ms. Burkhart.

Aha for Bobby Hedrick
who spies the cypress
slab before Emily Parks—
the queen loses today.

Only briefly do they ponder
the nameless girl their own age
who died on the ship home
and still bobs in a rum keg.

They turn out the trinkets
chosen last night or just now:
Betty Spaghetty doll, stuffed porpoise,
half-empty pouch of Sour Worms,

broken sand dollar, voucher for
free Ice Dream at Chick-Fil-A.
Corey Suggs drops up his homework
not caring he'll get a zero tomorrow.

Time for a picnic, says Ms. Burkhart
sneaking a peanut butter sandwich
to Eddie Green, whose mother
never remembers.

Only Macey Barefoot mourns
the rum keg girl, scribbles a
note she tucks under a rock.
Hope you feel better now.

How to See a Ghost

Don't read up on the occult and
linger around those reputedly haunted places
expecting to hear the whispers of soldiers
planning an ambush or the sobs
of women mourning their dead children
and the creak of old rocking chairs.

Don't ask the docent at those houses
if she has ever heard strange noises.
Either she has or she hasn't but she
probably won't tell you.
Instead she'll look away, annoyed,
thinking you're just one of *those people*.

If you really want to see a ghost,
do none of those things.
Do nothing.
Nothing at all.

Be like two ordinary people, God-fearing, practical people
with no interest in the supernatural whatsoever
who, while driving home one night
along a road they had traveled hundreds of times,
passed through a white mist
with a sad little face.

Although they did not believe in such things
they instantly knew it was a ghost
because when they drove on,
the sadness lingered, filling
the void between them.

The ghost didn't cackle,
it had no message.
And just as suddenly,
it was gone.

I'll tell you something else
because I know you'll ask.
It was the clearest of nights, no rain, no fog,
no crows and no owls circled overhead.
There wasn't even a full moon.
There was nothing special about it at all.

Too Bad You Were Never Mine

A wild cat snarls on linen now sleek with wear
the cover of Dot Perry's *Hill Life* from 1948
a year she, as Class Historian, says will go down
in history for Chapel Hill's new skating rink.

Good luck to the best GIRL basketball player,
says Jimmy Lovingood. *Nice jitter-bugger,*
swell gal wrote Doodle Hayes. *Save some men*
for me!!! cried Jeweldine Curtis.

In her picture, Dot's long dark hair sweeps
to the side, face tilts up, MGM eyes dream.
Forever Alice in the Drama Club debut
of *You Can't Take It With You.*

Popular but not voted the Valentine Queen,
the crown nabbed by Kathryn Ann Tuck,
chided for flirtatious ways, envied for curls,
languid smile and those deadly dimples.

Lots of luck to you Dot scrawled
Doug "Mouse" Sanders on the last page.
Remember that May Day Dance?
Too bad you were never mine.

Tucked inside is a picture of the 30 seniors
who made it to the 35th reunion in 1983.
Dot Perry Blankenship glows in the center
black chiffon softens hips wider than before.

A 2016 obituary found online ticks off a teaching
career and Dot's love for Bill, who went first,
a grief endured by a quick wit, green thumb,
and devotion to three blessed children.

Was it Denise? Pam? Perhaps it was Bill, Jr.,
harried executor, who tossed *Hill Life* into a box
of detritus that he loaded into the *Junque Shop* truck
then flicked his hand to the driver. *Thanks man.*

Best Price Sin Town

The night of our rampage
three good girls nudged
the s in *Prices* on the message
board for Mike's Tire & Muffler
just one space over, giving
the Lutherans something else
to pray about on Sunday.

Still itching, we decided to roll
toilet paper around the house
of Sally McRae, the judge's daughter,
a classmate we now hated
because she lied to us

pretended a stranger
who died in a car crash
had been her boyfriend, stowed
the *Tribune* clipping in her dorky purse
blotted dry eyes

the same girl who taught herself
to sign even though none of us
knew a deaf kid, just showing off,
we thought, another failure
to fit in.

The paper, stolen from Hardees,
just waffled through the air
too cheap to wrap around
anything but a dogwood tree
and we trembled, not bold enough
to throw the roll over the house
like the cool kids did.

Someone's beagle brayed
and lights flipped on
then a man stood on the porch
more father than judge
Who's there, who's there?
and we remembered
his frailty, shamed

by the wobble
in his voice.

Sally's light popped
on next so we ran
back to our Sunbird
drove home to empty
houses, our own parents
still at the country club
where they blurred the ragged
edges of their lives with love affairs
and brown-bagged gin.

Now that we've grown,
moved away from Sin Town,
we're the ones who lie,
fail to fit in, and the rare times
we three see each other,
we never talk about that night
instead one of us says
*we must get together
one day,* someone else
says *really we must,*
but then a phone buzzes
or a child tugs at our arm
and we glide away, back
to the safety of our lies.

Additional Acknowledgments

The poet would also like to thank:

The North Carolina Poetry Society and poet Sandra Beasley for selecting "Eulogy of a Northern Red Oak" as a finalist for the 2019 Poet Laureate Award;

My fellow poets Ruth Moose and Mary Barnard for their wisdom and guidance;

Leah Maines and the team at Finishing Line Press for their faith in me;

Caroline Becker for cheerfully agreeing to be photographed for the cover;

and the wood thrush, the best musician I know… undoubtedly the instrument of God.

Waiting for the Wood Thrush is the first poetry collection by **Ashley Memory**. She draws her inspiration from the beauty of the ancient Uwharrie mountains surrounding her home in rural Randolph County, North Carolina, where she lives with her sculptor husband, Johnpaul Harris. When she's not musing on a metaphor, she's either brewing raspberry jam or poking around an abandoned cemetery imagining the lives of the people sleeping under her feet. She and Johnpaul share their home with three rescued pets, the dogs Buster and Finn and Little Puss the cat—although they see themselves as the rescuers rather than the other way around.

Memory's writing has appeared in many publications, including *CAIRN, Eureka Literary Review, Wildlife in North Carolina, The Thomas Wolfe Review, Romantic Homes,* and *Raleigh News & Observer,* and her poems have recently appeared in *Pinesong, Broad River Review, Gyroscope Review, Naugatuck River Review, Coffin Bell, Turnpike,* and *The Phoenix*. Her writing has been nominated for a Pushcart Prize and she has twice won the Doris Betts Fiction Prize sponsored by the NC Writers' Network.

In 2011, Ingalls Publishing Group published her novel, *Naked and Hungry,* which was a finalist for the James Jones First Novel Fellowship and listed as one of the season's most promising debut novels by *Library Journal*. Reviewer Linda Brinson, *Greensboro News & Record*: "Memory knows her territory. She gets the details of 21st-century small-town North Carolina right. She obviously enjoys poking a little fun at such staples as good ol' boys, restless housewives, hypocritical preachers and slickly crooked politicians. The humor isn't too heavy-handed, however, and as a result, the book is really funny."

A former communications director at the University of North Carolina at Chapel Hill, Memory currently teaches creative writing at Central Carolina Community College in Pittsboro, NC and the Charlotte Center for Literary Arts in Charlotte, NC.

www.ingramcontent.com/pod-product-compliance
Lightning Source LLC
LaVergne TN
LVHW041558070426
835507LV00011B/1175